Looking at FRANCE

R. J. HARRISON CHURCH

Ronald Harrison Church has a real affection for the beautiful country of France which he knows so well. He enjoys meeting its people, he appreciates its way of life and the variety of its scenery, and he takes great pleasure in the fine cooking for which France is famous.

Every region of France has its own individuality—in ways of living, customs, scenery and type of food. The author describes them in detail, pointing the contrasts between the snowy heights of the Alps and the rich farmlands of Normandy, between the Basque country with its own language and Paris, between the resorts of the warm sunny Mediterranean coast and the industrial towns of the north. He describes the people—their homes, schools and pastimes—and tells us something of the past as well as of France's great achievements in the present.

His book is illustrated with scores of superb photographs, many taken specially for it.

almost every town and district.

Some of the photographs in this book are from his own collection. Many others are by Jonathan Rutland, an experienced photographer and author of the companion volumes *Looking at Denmark* and *Looking at Israel*.

Looking at FRANCE

Street market
in the Paris suburbs

Looking at

R. J. HARRISON CHURCH

Adam and Charles Black   London
J. B. Lippincott Company   Philadelphia and New York

Bléré, Loire Valley

FRANCE

Looking at Other Countries

Looking at HOLLAND
Looking at ITALY
Looking at GREECE
Looking at NORWAY
Looking at ISRAEL
Looking at DENMARK
Looking at JAPAN
Looking at SPAIN
Looking at FRANCE

Further titles in preparation

Grateful acknowledgement is made to the following for their permission to reproduce photographs:

Air France 11a
Margaret Baker 27a and b, 28a and b, 30a
Editions Bias 30b and c (from *Maisons Paysannes de France*)
Vincent Brown 1, 13, 17a, 58b
J. Allan Cash 20b, 24, 36a
La Documentation Française 17b, 40c, 63 (Viguier-Tourisme)
R. J. Harrison Church 11b, 26, 47b, 50, 55b
French Government Tourist Office 9a, 12, 16, 18, 20a, 31a and b, 32a and b, 34, 35b, 37a and b, 40a and b, 41, 42a, 43a, 45, 47a, 48, 49a and b, 51, 52a and b, 53, 54a and b, 60a
Keystone Press 21, 22a and b, 59
Office de Documentation par le Film 22c
Radio Times Hulton Picture Library 60b, 61
Jonathan Rutland 3, 5, 7b, 8, 14a and b, 15a, b and c, 19, 23, 25, 33, 35a, 36b, 38a and b, 39a and b, 42b, 43b, 44, 46, 55a and c, 56a and b, 57, 58a
SNCF 10
SNPA photo collection 9b
Dr. I. B. Thompson 6
Fiona Wilkie 7a
Thomas A. Wilkie Co. Ltd. 29
Tourist Photo Library Ltd. 62

The photographs on the book jacket are by Ciganovic (top) and Jonathan Rutland

The maps are by H. Johns

SBN 7136 1016 6

LIBRARY OF CONGRESS CATALOG CARD NUMBER: 70:97797
PRINTED IN GREAT BRITAIN BY *JARROLD & SONS LTD. NORWICH*

CONTENTS

The unit of currency is the *franc*. £1 is worth about 13 francs. $1 is worth about 5½ francs

Savoy Alps

The Country

France is a country of varied and beautiful scenery, a country with magnificent cathedrals and art treasures. The French are famous for their food and wines, clever scientists and engineers, and have a reputation for being witty and logical.

France is just half an hour across the English Channel by hovercraft from Britain, a few hours across the Atlantic by jet, and shares its borders with six other European countries. Until modern roads and railways were built through the Alps, the Rhône-Saône valley was the easiest way from Italy to northern Europe, so France has always been the meeting place of Mediterranean and northern peoples.

France is unusually compact. Apart from two peninsulas jutting out in the northwest, the country is roughly square, giving it a short coastline for its size. This has saved much expense in building roads and railways, compared with elongated countries such as Norway. France is also the only country with coasts on the English Channel, the North Sea, the Atlantic and the Mediterranean.

Combourg in Brittany

After the U.S.S.R. France is the largest country in Europe. It is over twice as large as the United Kingdom, but would fit comfortably into the state of Texas. Most of the northern half and western side is lowland, making farming possible and transport easy. The highlands and mountains are in the south-central part and along the southwestern, southeastern and eastern borders.

Amiens on voting day. The cathedral is in the background

A small farm in southwestern France

France has much fertile land and, especially in the south, many sunny days. Most of France gets enough rain, without having the excessive moisture and cloud of some northern lands. Therefore natural conditions are good for growing many kinds of crops.

However, French farming rarely makes the best use of the land. There are large and very productive farms around Paris, but elsewhere they are mostly small and inefficient.

In the middle and south of France the farmers are peasants, who own small farms. When they die their farms have usually been divided among their sons, so the farms become smaller and smaller. These farms often have many separated strips, since, to be fair to each son, the fertile and less fertile fields have each been equally divided. Working around to each strip wastes much time, and machinery cannot be used efficiently. So the French government is encouraging *remembrement*, or the consolidation of scattered strips.

Once a farmer has a compact farm and the loan of money, he can buy machines such as tractors and harrows, he can put fertilizers on his land more quickly and he can grade and pack his crops better.

Handpainting Sèvres porcelain

France is famous for its manufactured goods, and hand industries of the past still exist, such as Gobelins tapestries and Sèvres porcelain.

Most industry began in the northern part of the country, because the only large coalfield is near the Belgian border, and during the nineteenth century it was largely confined to this area. But the twentieth century hydro-electric power stations have been built in the mountains and on the Rhine and Rhône rivers. Since World War II oil and gas have been developed, at home and in the Algerian Sahara. One long pipeline links towns between Marseilles and Strasbourg, and natural gas is piped over most of France.

Consequently modern industries using these new sources of power have grown up away from the coalfields, in such cities as Paris, Toulouse and Grenoble.

Petro-chemical works are in the ports where oil is brought in, on pipelines, or at Lacq, in southwestern France, the source of most natural gas.

Part of the natural gas factory
at Lacq

9

French railways (*Société Nationale des Chemins de fer Français—*
SNCF) are famous for fast trains and good time-keeping.
They were largely rebuilt because of tremendous war damage.
Lines with the most traffic are electrified. The famous *Mistral*
express covers the 195 miles from Paris to Dijon in 2 hours
20 minutes at an average speed of 84 mph and reaches
Marseilles, 536 miles from Paris with four stops in 6 hours
40 minutes. The *Capitole* from Paris to Toulouse reaches 125
mph on one stretch.

French railways were early users of Diesel multiple-coach
trains or *michelines*, so called because the Michelin company
first built them. Gas-turbine trains will soon be introduced
on the Paris–Cherbourg line.

France has more roads for its area than any other country in
the world, but most are too narrow and bumpy for modern
traffic. So France has begun to build *autoroutes* similar to the
British motorways or American highways. The *Autoroute de
l'Esterel* avoiding Cannes, and the *Autoroute du Nord* (Paris–
Lille) are the main ones. Others are being built from Paris to
the Mediterranean and from Paris to Rouen.

The *Mistral*

Caravelle jets at Orly
airport, Paris

France was a pioneer in air travel. *Air France* is Europe's largest aviation company, and has the world's longest network of flights. Paris Orly is one of Europe's leading airports, and there will soon be a new large one on the northeast side of the city.

Before the French Revolution France was divided into provinces, some much larger than others. These were abolished in 1789 and the country was divided into 90 *départements* or counties of roughly equal size. There are now five more since the growth of Paris necessitated splitting up two of the *départements* into seven. Each has a number according to its alphabetical order and these are used for car registration and sorting letters. The names of the old provinces, such as Normandy and Brittany, are still commonly used to describe the regions of France.

The car on the left has 29 on its registration number. This is the number of the *département* of Finistère in Brittany

Paris

Paris is a wonderful, fascinating city. It has theatres, cinemas, concert halls, opera houses, night clubs, museums and art galleries. Its department stores and fashion houses attract shoppers, and Paris University draws students from all over the world. The tourist is awestruck by the flying buttresses and stained glass of Notre Dame cathedral, charmed by the little streets of Montmartre, thrilled by the view from the Eiffel Tower. The gardens and wide boulevards give a feeling of space and freedom, while the solid stone buildings (there are few modern glass and concrete blocks in the middle of the city) give a sense of history.

But Paris is not just a beautiful tourist attraction. It is the seat of government and the headquarters of the civil service. Two and three quarter million people live in the city proper with a further six million in the suburbs. Most French firms try to have an office in the city. Thousands of factories of all descriptions are to be found in the city and in the suburbs, which grew up in the nineteenth and twentieth centuries.

Paris was settled about 300 BC when the Parisii made their homes on an island in the Seine now called Ile de la Cité. The Romans conquered them in 52 BC and named the town Lutetia. Villas were built and vines planted around them on the drier hill to the south on the left bank of the Seine; the arena the Romans built there is now used as a children's playground.

In AD 450 Paris was attacked by Huns from the north, but they were successfully beaten off under the leadership of Geneviève, who later became the patron saint of Paris. The southern hill is still called La Montagne Sainte-Geneviève.

Notre Dame cathedral was begun in 1163 and was completed by 1330. The first royal palace was built nearby. In it is the lovely Sainte Chapelle whose lofty windows of thirteenth-century stained glass tell the Bible story in 1134 panes. Now the Ile de la Cité also houses the headquarters of the police and the law courts.

St. Michel bridge

In 1253 Robert de Sorbon founded a college, the first of what is now Paris University, bringing new life to the left bank of the Seine. It became known as the *quartier latin* (Latin Quarter) because teaching and ordinary speech at the university were in Latin instead of French.

Paris grew and new walls were built in 1370 on the north side. The Louvre, first built as a fortress in the thirteenth century, was gradually transformed into a palace. After the Revolution in the eighteenth century it was turned into a museum and art gallery, and wings were added in the nineteenth century. The nearby Tuileries Palace, begun for the Queen Mother Catherine de Médicis in the sixteenth century, was burnt down in 1871 but its gardens remain. Like other French public gardens, these are typically formal with straight gravel paths, trees in parallel lines and geometrically shaped flowerbeds. This part of Paris was royal Paris and nearby are the great fashion houses, *parfumiers* and jewellers, whose predecessors served the royal court.

Louis XIV spent most of his time 14 miles away from Paris at Versailles, the largest and most sumptuous palace of all French palaces, set in the grandest gardens. In Paris Louis XIV had earlier city walls demolished, replacing them with boulevards. The Invalides, the hospital for wounded and old soldiers, was also built during his reign.

The Louvre

Silhouette artist in the Tuileries

14

There are many stalls selling paintings
and books on the Left Bank

Café on the Champs Elysées: Arc de Triomphe

The famous triumphal arch, the Arc de Triomphe, was begun
in Napoleon I's reign. From it twelve roads radiate outwards
and downwards, and so the hill is known as the Etoile or
"star". From it are many fine views, including the impressive
one down France's most famous avenue, the Champs
Elysées, through the spacious and beautiful Place de la
Concorde, with its fountains and arches, and on to the
Tuileries gardens.

Baron Haussmann, appointed chief administrator of Paris by
Napoleon III, did most to give the city its spacious character
and clear street plan. He put the finishing touches to the
Champs Elysées and Place de la Concorde, built the Place
de l'Opéra and the Place de la République, enlarged the
Grands Boulevards between them, and added seven of the
twelve roads radiating from the Arc de Triomphe. He also
laid out two areas of woods and open spaces, the Bois de
Boulogne at the west end of Paris and the Bois de Vincennes
in the east. Paris's most famous landmark, the Eiffel Tower,
was designed for the Paris Exhibition of 1889 by Gustave
Eiffel.

Palace of Versailles

Watching the traffic from a café

In comparison with London or New York, Paris has a far greater number of people living near their work in the city in tall apartment houses. Because of this and because few employers provide canteens or cafeterias, many Parisians go home to lunch. This causes a rush hour in the middle of the day as well as morning and evening. Most travel by bus or *Métro* (underground). Passengers enter buses at the rear and in most they leave by another door at the front. The conductor, who stands or sits by the entry door, tells a passenger how many "sections" long is his journey. The passenger then gives him that number of perforated tickets from a *carnet* of twenty tickets he can buy on any bus. As road congestion is bad many people take the Métro. Like the New York subway, this has a set fare, regardless of distance, and is cheaper than the buses except for short journeys. The network of tracks is denser and the stations closer than in London, but unlike the London Underground, few lines reach the suburbs. Travellers to the suburbs must take suburban buses or go by main line trains.

Much money is being spent on improving transport facilities. A new 60 mph underground railway with more widely-spaced stations is being built to link the east and west suburbs with the city. New roads along each bank of the Seine help the flow of traffic, and a highway is being constructed round the city boundary (*le périphérique*).

Tickets such as these can be used on the Métro or the bus

Parisian street entertainer:
a fire eater

Paris has characteristic districts, often former villages, which are typified by what goes on or who lives in them. There is the boisterous, entertainment-providing Montmartre, and elegant Auteuil; Montparnasse is a district of writers and artists, like Chelsea in London or Greenwich Village in New York.

The capital also has important industries. Some larger factories are down the river, such as the Renault works at Boulogne-Billancourt. Others are on the flat St. Denis plain on the north side of Paris. Some depend in part upon goods carried by barge on the rivers and canals that make a network over the country.

By AD 2000 Paris will almost certainly have 12 million inhabitants—and could have twice as many. There are building restrictions on new industry and offices in Paris. Other towns are being helped to provide more jobs and homes to attract people to them instead of to the capital. Meanwhile, parts of Paris are being rebuilt and huge apartment blocks have gone up, especially in the suburbs.

Flats on the
outskirts of Paris

Chenonceaux

Around Paris—
Châteaux and Champagne

Paris is at the hub of a region of flat or gently undulating country, through which the river Seine flows. This part of France is known as the Paris Basin. There are no mountains, so transportation is easy, the soil is good for farming and there are many industries.

The area immediately round Paris is the Ile-de-France. It got its name from the Franks, a Germanic tribe who settled here after the Romans left France. The power of the Franks gradually spread, and from them grew the nation of France. Most of the Ile-de-France was once covered with forests, and some large patches still remain, such as those at Fontainebleau and Chantilly.

These and many other places have fine *châteaux* (large country houses), which were often built as hunting lodges for the king and aristocracy. In 1661 Fouquet, Louis XIV's Minister of Finance, entertained the king at his new château at Vaux-la-Vicomte. It was so magnificent that the king was enraged. He threw Fouquet into prison and employed his ex-minister's architect, decorator and landscape gardener, together with an army of workmen, to build him an even more magnificent château at Versailles.

There are many châteaux in France, but the best known ones are along the beautiful Loire and its tributaries. Many of the châteaux were built four or five hundred years ago at a time when the Hundred Years War forced the French kings out of Paris. Châteaux were built as homes for the king and his courtiers and as strongholds. Later smaller châteaux such as Chenonceaux were built as country homes.

The château of Chinon had been a fortress for hundreds of years when, in 1427, Charles VII, chased out of Paris by Henry IV of England, came there with his court. It was here that he received Joan of Arc, who spurred him on against the English. Chinon is a perfect example of a feudal castle and a medieval town—yet nearby is one of France's latest nuclear power stations.

The ultimate in glory and extravagance is the château of Chambord. It has 440 rooms and two intertwined yet separate stone staircases. No wonder that it took 1800 men fifteen years to build!

Tours is the best headquarters for visiting the châteaux. As the burial place of St. Martin it was for centuries a stopping place for pilgrims on the way to Spain. Later it became important for the manufacture of silk.

Château de Chambord

Typical French road bordered by trees

The district between Paris and the river Loire is called Beauce. The roads are lined with trees, as is common in France, and run straight for mile after mile. There are no hedges, so the view stretches to the horizon over flat fields of wheat, barley and maize (corn).

The farms of Beauce are large and prosperous. France is the only country in Western Europe to produce much more wheat than it needs, and the surplus is exported.

Long ago water was very difficult to obtain in Beauce, for very deep wells had to be sunk to reach it. Because of this, market towns such as Chartres and Orleans grew up on the fringes of Beauce. Chartres has one of the world's most beautiful cathedrals, famous for its long stone statues and for the 600-year-old stained glass windows. Orleans is perhaps best known as the town which was freed from the English by Joan of Arc—this event is celebrated every year, on May 8th.

Southeast of Paris lies Brie, another fertile area with large farms growing barley for feeding dairy cattle, whose milk is used to make Brie cheese.

The front of Chartres cathedral

La Champagne, which means "the plain", is the name of another region—while *le* champagne is its famous wine. The main town, Reims, has a lovely cathedral, specially designed for coronations, and almost all French kings were crowned there.

Champagne, drunk on festive occasions throughout the world, comes from grapes grown between Reims and Epernay. Miles of tunnels have been carved out of the chalk rock, about 100 feet down, and it is here that the grapes are crushed and the champagne made and stored. One firm has over eleven miles of cellars and twenty-five million bottles stored there.

Champagne is a blend of wines of different years from various vineyards. Nearly all other good-quality French wine comes from an individual vineyard and type of vine, and one year's juice is not mixed with another. It is local variations in soil, weather and type of vine, together with the wine-maker's care, that lead to the wide range of distinctive wines for which France is famous. In making champagne, white and black grapes are crushed as soon as they are brought in from the many small vineyards. After crushing, the pulp is separated from the liquid, which is then left in barrels until it ferments into wine.

Champagne
cellar at Epernay

Harvesting the grapes in a champagne vineyard

After the sediment is thrown out, the bottles are topped up with wine and corked

Old wine sweetened with sugar is then added before bottling to cause a second fermentation which produces the famous bubbles. This process was probably discovered by a Benedictine monk, Dom Pérignon, who lived from 1638 to 1715. The bottles are stored at an angle of 45 degrees in racks, and they are turned slightly every day or so to drain the sediment down to the cork. The bottles have a white spot on their base to help the cellarman gauge the right amount of turning.

When all the sediment has settled by the cork, the bottles go upside down across a freezing bath, which freezes the sediment into a lump. When the cork is removed the sediment is thrown out by the gas in the wine. The bottle is then topped-up and corked. Champagne is stored for from two to five years, and this and the many processes involved make it a costly wine.

At the Feast of St. John, the champagne firms invite all those who help to make the wine and their families to the cellars. As the bottles are opened to serve the guests the noise is like a fireworks show.

Operating a wine press

Northern France and its Industry

In the western part of the Paris Basin is Normandy, with the river Seine cutting across it in wide loops. To the south and west of the Seine, many cows are grazed on the fine pastures. Their milk is made into the famous Isigny butter, and such well-known cheeses as Camembert and Pont L'Evêque, named after the small towns in which they are made. Marie Harel, who perfected the Camembert cheese-making process, is said to have been given shavings of wood by a coffin maker with which to pack her cheese. Today this cheese is still sold in round boxes of very thin wood.

Normandy also has many apple trees, and cider is made. Some of the cider is distilled into Calvados, a spirit which has the same name as the *département* in which it is made.

It was on the Normandy beaches at Arromanches and at Omaha Bay that the Allies made their tremendous landings on June 6th, 1944, during the liberation of Western Europe in World War II. Around the Cotentin peninsula, the coast becomes wild and rocky. Near where it joins the equally rugged coast of Brittany is Mont-Saint-Michel, the twelfth-century monastery perched on top of a tiny granite island.

Mont-Saint-Michel

Le Havre

Le Havre at the mouth of the Seine is France's second most important seaport after Marseilles. French trade with America led to its birth and Le Havre grew rapidly when steamships developed this commerce. The docks were destroyed in World War II but have since been rebuilt, and all but the world's largest tankers and liners can berth here. Oil refineries, automobile and other factories are gradually occupying the mud flats to the east of the city.

Nearly 80 miles up the Seine is Rouen, the capital of Normandy and a busy port. There has been a town here since pre-Roman times, and it was in the market place of Rouen that Joan of Arc was burned to death in 1431. The beautiful cathedral has a butter tower, so called because it was built with the money paid by people who "bought" a dispensation from the Church to eat butter in Lent. Rouen today is one of the chief manufacturing and industrial cities of France. It has an oil refinery, cotton spinning, steel, chemical and paper industries, and also manufactures electric cables, clothing and other textiles.

Picardy and Artois lie between Normandy and the Belgian border. There are sandy beaches along this coastline with resorts such as fashionable Le Touquet. Boulogne is the biggest fishing port of France and both it and Calais are cross-Channel terminals for passenger services from England. Dunkirk is capable of taking large ships and is becoming increasingly important for its steel and shipbuilding industries, which use imported iron ore and coal from the Franco-Belgian coalfield.

Picardy lies in gentle slopes around the Somme river. It has large farms, and on its rich soil cereals, sugar beets and potatoes are grown and there is good pasture for cattle. Black peat, similar to that of the English Fens, has formed in the marshy valleys, where there are tiny but rich vegetable farms which are reached by boat. Here is Amiens with its picturesque market-on-the-water where many streams meet.

Artois has a long ridge of higher land bordering the flat plain of Flanders with its very small farms and centuries-old textile industries. Here are the towns of Cambrai, which gave its name to cambric, and Arras, famed for its tapestries.

Model-boat enthusiasts at Amiens. International races are held here

To the north is France's main coalfield and here has developed the great industrial area formed by the three cities of Lille, Roubaix and Tourcoing, with their iron, steel and chemical industries and large textile mills.

Another great industrial area of northern France has grown up around Thionville in Lorraine, further to the east. Nine-tenths of the iron ore mined in France comes from this district and forms the basis of a great steel industry. Coal, mined on the border with the German Saar, and salt found to the southeast of Nancy, are also used in Lorraine's chemical works. Yet there are still some old craft industries—the cut or crystal glass of Baccarat and the stringed musical instruments of Mirecourt.

Nancy, the capital of Lorraine, has a famous large square known as Place Stanislas. It is named after Stanislas, the last Duke of Lorraine, who laid out this square to the glory of Louis XV and had many fine buildings erected round it. In an elegant café in the square, people linger over coffee, the local beer (brewing is another important industry of Lorraine) or *mirabelle*, a drink made from the small yellow plums of Lorraine. Nearby one can buy *bergamotes*, a local sweet or candy made from lemon and honey.

Barge on a canal south of Cambrai

Shopping in the market

Preparing lunch

People and Homes

French people are generally polite and courteous. It takes some time for two people of the same sex to pass through several doors, for at each one the French person will insist you go first. When you insist that he or she shall go first, you find that much parleying and determination is needed. But life in the cities has brushed away some of the politeness. The French have never taken to queuing or forming lines, and getting into a bus or train is almost a free-for-all. An attempt has been made to solve this problem by working out a system of entry tickets, with priorities for the wounded, the infirm and expectant mothers.

People entering a bar, café or restaurant will greet those sitting nearby with a nod, saying *"Messieurs"* or *"Mesdames"*. Similar greetings are exchanged again when leaving, and likewise when people pass in a corridor or on a staircase. At work, colleagues will shake hands every morning and on leaving in the evening. Long-parted Frenchmen will hug each other with great feeling. Frenchmen kiss women relatives three times on alternate cheeks; a lady who is not a relative but is much respected is kissed on the fingers of her hand.

A French family is usually a closely knit unit. Parents command respect, and all members kiss one another in the morning and on going to bed. There are certain times during the year when wider family reunions take place, such as at Christmas, the New Year, First Communion, birthdays and on national holidays. On these occasions there will be a fine meal with many courses and different wines. Even young children will often have a little watered red wine.

Breakfast is usually coffee and a bread roll. The main meals are taken at mid-day and in the evening. An everyday lunch or dinner will consist of soup or hors d'œuvres, followed by vegetables and meat (served together or separately) and rounded off by cheese, fresh fruit or a light dessert (no filling pies or puddings!). Delicious light crusty bread is eaten with everything but the fruit and dessert. Cheap red wine is drunk throughout the meal. For special occasions extra courses such as fish will be added, and cheese, fruit and dessert will all be eaten.

The French are very proud of their cooking and spend a lot on food. Every region or town has its own speciality in food or drink. But steak and chips (french fried potatoes) or pork chops and French beans can be found in restaurants all over France. And as more and more housewives go out to work, canned and packaged foods are becoming more popular.

A game of *boules*

The café, open to the pavement or sidewalk in summer, glassed in during winter, is a great French institution. You are as welcome whether you want an alcoholic or non-alcoholic drink, with or without something to eat, and are an adult or child, man or woman. People often meet their friends in cafés or restaurants.

Every Sunday in summer and on holidays, many families flock out of the cities to the nearest wood, lake or seaside resort. Many drive out by car, set up camping chairs and table and have a well-prepared cold lunch with wine and coffee. In the afternoon they sleep off the meal, turn on the radio or play *boules*, a bowling game, using heavy metal bowls and played on any fairly level piece of ground.

For holidays or vacations more and more French families go to a "second" or "holiday" home—usually a small house in a seaside or country spot. Camping in multi-sectioned large and gaily coloured tents is also popular. Special French developments are the *Colonies de Vacances* for children only—camps or holiday homes with organized activities—and the *Club Méditerranée* where people live informally in simple shacks by the sea, wear little and eat well. Until after World War II the French rarely went abroad for holidays but now they also seek the sun in countries farther south.

29

Parisian apartment house

There are great contrasts between old and new, town and country houses. Along Parisian and other city streets, in the middle of the towns, are the characteristic apartment blocks, usually six floors high. They are entered by an inconspicuous door, usually leading to a courtyard with stairways at each corner. Through lace-covered glass doors the *concierge*, or caretaker, inspects all passers-by and usually knows everything about the various residents. Most Parisians live in these blocks. Many taller new apartment blocks are now being built in the suburbs. There are few well-planned suburbs of individual houses and gardens, so characteristic of America and Britain.

Outside the cities, people live in houses and cottages. Those on the Franco-Belgian coalfield are built of brick, those in the Loire Valley are white-walled, slate-roofed and ivy covered, while in Alsace there are beautiful gabled timber houses decorated with window boxes and hanging baskets of flowers.

Most dwellings are light grey, though gay colours are becoming more popular, and windows are often shuttered. Many houses have high railings with lockable gates. A Frenchman's home truly is his castle.

MIDDLE House in Provence
BELOW Farm in Dauphiné

Alsace and the Vosges

Where it forms the frontier between France and Germany, the Rhine is a large river flowing through a flat, wide valley. This is bounded by high rolling hills: the Black Forest on the German side and the Vosges on the French.

Along the steep edge of the Vosges there are vineyards and such beautiful villages as Obernai, Riquewihr and Kaysersberg. The lovely old market town of Colmar lies in the plain and it is here that Bartholdi, sculptor of the Statue of Liberty in New York, was born.

Early in the Franco-Prussian war of 1870–71, Alsace was taken by the Germans, who continued to occupy it until the end of World War I in 1918. Many buildings and names show German influence and the people of eastern Alsace speak a kind of German.

Strasbourg: "La Petite France"

Strasbourg, or "fort of the road", grew up on an island in the river Ill on the great trading route from the Mediterranean to the Baltic. Many centuries later Gutenberg, an inventor of printing, lived here from 1424 to 1444, and in 1792 Rouget de L'Isle, a volunteer soldier and a musician, composed in one night the French national anthem, the *Marseillaise*.

Strasbourg: the fine timbered house is called Maison Kammerzell

People put platforms on the roofs of their houses for the storks

Strasbourg has a beautiful cathedral, built of pink sandstone from the northern Vosges, with a tall spire and a remarkable astronomical clock. There are many beautiful timbered houses in Strasbourg, especially in the area of *La Petite France* alongside a canal. Many houses here, and in other towns and villages of Alsace, have storks' nests on their roofs. The stork is a symbol of Alsace: people encourage the birds by fixing a platform for them to build their nest on.

Strasbourg is a busy river port and an industrial city with important engineering, steel, chemical and shipbuilding industries. It is near the middle of the European Economic Community (or Common Market) and is the seat of the Council of Europe or parliament of eighteen European countries.

West of Strasbourg is the narrow Saverne gap through the Vosges, with barely enough room for the canal, railway and road to Paris. To the south of it is the highest part of the Vosges. The mountains have forests on their steep slopes but the summits are rounded and grassy. People ski here in winter, and in spring and summer cows are pastured, driven up the mountains by cowmen or *marcaires* who make Munster or Géromé cheese.

Lac de Guéry

The Massif Central

High, rocky and windswept, the Massif Central is an obstacle to transport. It is also the source of many rivers, for example the Loire, and a source of hydro-electric power from large dams which have been built on the Dordogne and the Truyère rivers.

Many small coalfields have been worked but the important ones are along the eastern edge of the massif at St. Etienne and Le Creusot where heavy industry has been developed. Formerly gold, copper and tin were mined from the ancient rocks of the Massif Central, and decorative metal ware was made at Limoges. But the metals have been used up and the craftsmen now make beautiful Limoges pottery. Not far away is Aubusson, famous for its superb tapestries—the one hanging in the new Coventry cathedral in England was made there.

The main town, Clermont-Ferrand, is in the most fertile part of the region and is the home of the Michelin company, famous for the manufacture of rubber tires. This company employs many thousands of people, in France and elsewhere.

33

To the west of Clermont-Ferrand are the Monts Dômes. These are extinct, well-preserved volcanoes. Pavin and many other lakes in the area are volcanic craters which have been filled with water, while others such as Chambon and Aydat were formed when lava from erupting volcanoes blocked a river valley. A little to the south are the rugged remains of a much larger but more eroded volcano, the Puy de Sancy.

South of the Puy de Sancy, near Murat, is Europe's largest extinct and exploded volcano, the Cantal. The Plomb du Cantal, which rises to nearly 6000 feet, is part of the gigantic crater left by the volcano when it exploded. It takes a day to walk round the edge. Inside the crater are rich pastures, and the milk from the cattle is used to make Cantal, St. Nectaire and Bleu d'Auvergne cheeses. Cantal cheese is made by the cowmen in their *burons* (summer huts) on the high pastures.

The town of St. Flour is on a headland at the southeastern end of one of the Cantal's former lava flows. South of it is the lofty Garabit viaduct, carrying a railway across the deep Truyère valley. The experience Eiffel gained in building the viaduct helped him to build his famous tower in Paris.

Folk dancing at St. Flour

34

Garabit viaduct

The town of Le Puy on the Loire has the remains of three volcanoes. Their craters and cones have been worn away, leaving only stumps, two of them needle-like. One of these is crowned by an eleventh-century chapel, and on another is a huge statue of the Virgin, cast from 213 cannons captured by the French army in the Crimean War. On the third, more level stump or mound is the cathedral built with volcanic stone of several colours. Pilgrims came here to sleep on a stone slab, praying to be cured upon waking. When in the twelfth century brigands attacked the pilgrims, a group of crusaders banded together to stop them. They were dressed in white hoods, and are commemorated each year in the Feast of the Assumption procession.

Le Puy: the eleventh-century chapel

Because of all the volcanic activity there are many thermal springs in the area, and people with various illnesses come to spas such as Vichy and Le Mont Dore for treatment with the waters. At Chaudes-Aigues the hot springs are used for central heating, cooking, washing wool in a local industry and for incubating eggs.

35

The Causses is a 3000-foot-high plateau, and over the ages the two rivers, Lot and Tarn, have cut canyons through it—smaller but almost as impressive as Colorado's Grand Canyon. The pastureland in the area is just sufficient to nourish sheep, whose milk is made into Roquefort cheese. Many lambs are killed at birth and their perfect skins are used to make gloves at nearby Millau.

Most of the farmers are very poor, and many have given up farming. Their farmhouses have been converted and are used as weekend or holiday homes for the ever-increasing number of tourists who come here to enjoy the good air and scenery, to take exciting trips through the Tarn gorges, or to ski in winter on the Puy de Sancy.

Most French people are Roman Catholics, but in the Cévennes on the high southeastern edge of the Massif Central there are many Protestants. In the seventeenth century Louis XIV attempted to destroy the Protestant faith, but many Protestants gathered in this rocky, hilly region where they could hide and defend themselves. Today many villages have a Protestant as well as a Catholic church, and some only a Protestant church.

Both Catholic and Protestant services are announced on this sign outside a small town

36

Stalactites and stalagmites at Padirac

Pigs are trained to search for truffles

Aquitaine

The Massif Central slopes down in the west to a wooded plateau, through which rivers have cut deep valleys. Many thousands of years ago, early man sheltered in the caves of these limestone cliffs. Les Eyzies, a village on the Vézère river, has been called the capital of prehistory—countless paintings by early man have been found nearby. Those of Lascaux are the finest of all. The caves at Padirac, close by, are of great interest; there you can take a boat trip on a river 338 feet below ground level through vast galleries adorned with stalactites and stalagmites.

The chestnut, walnut and pine woods provide nuts, edible oil, resin, timber and other products, but the most unusual product comes from the oak. Pigs and dogs are specially trained to smell out the truffles which grow on the roots of oak trees in this region. Truffles are an edible fungus and are a great and costly delicacy.

Around the Garonne river, in the heart of Aquitaine, are many quiet, beautiful little towns, gentle hills and rich farmlands. Some of the towns were *bastides* or fortress settlements in the wars between the French and the English. Montauban was the earliest French one, built in 1144, and Libourne the most famous English one, constructed in 1270.

It was during the three hundred years (1154–1453) when the lands around Bordeaux were English that trade developed in the rich red wines called claret. Most comes from the vineyards of Médoc, west of the Gironde estuary. Other well-known wines from around Bordeaux include Graves, Barsac and Sauternes. Bordeaux, Burgundy and Champagne are the three most important areas in France for the production of fine-quality wines.

In two areas in Aquitaine, wine is also distilled to produce brandy. The foremost area is around Cognac to the north of the Gironde, but there is also the Armagnac district to the south.

The coast south of the Gironde has glorious sandy beaches backed by high dunes and lagoons all the way to Biarritz. From there the coast becomes rocky, announcing the beginning of the Pyrenees mountains. Behind the dunes and extending as much as 60 miles inland is the Landes, which means "heath". This former wilderness of sand and marsh was

Libourne

Grape harvest in a Graves vineyard

reclaimed in the eighteenth and nineteenth centuries by planting pine trees, which today provide resin and timber for local paper factories.

A typical farmer near Marmande, southeast of Bordeaux, has eight acres. Each year he grows a succession of vegetables such as spring onions, lettuce, radishes, peas and haricot beans. He also grows tobacco and Italian tomatoes, whose bushy plants have pear-shaped fruit. The tobacco he dries and "cures" in a special well-ventilated barn. These crops are grown for sale and are sent to the market or railway station at Marmande.

Collecting resin from the pine trees

The farmer also grows some corn (maize) to feed his poultry, wheat to provide flour for bread, and vines to give him and his family red wine at every meal. But his family of many children must work hard the whole year round. They have never been away for a holiday or vacation.

Aquitaine is also renowned for its fisheries, both fresh and salt water. The clear rushing streams flowing down from the Pyrenees carry trout, salmon, gudgeon and pike. The world salmon-fishing championships are held at Navarrenx. On the coast at Saint-Jean-de-Luz is France's largest tuna-catching fleet, which goes as far south as West Africa for this mighty fish. At Hossegor, north of Saint-Jean-de-Luz and Biarritz, are some of France's most famous oyster beds.

Tobacco drying

39

Bordeaux and Toulouse are the only large towns of southwestern France. Bordeaux is the hub of the wine trade. Vast quantities are bottled here, and allied trades supply the bottles, corks, labels, barrels and crates. But Bordeaux has many other industries: wood and paper mills, cement, chemical and aircraft-component works.

The town is spacious, and its Place des Quinconces (zig-zags of trees) is Europe's largest square except for Red Square in Moscow.

Toulouse was once the capital of the Visigoths, who overran France in the fifth century. In the fourteenth and fifteenth centuries, it carried on a rich trade in woad, the ancient blue dye obtained from the plant woad which was grown around the city.

Toulouse is now best known for its aircraft industry. The *Caravelle*, the first jet airliner with engines at the rear, was built here. The Anglo-French supersonic *Concorde* is assembled here, and also near Bristol in England.

The *Concorde*

Breton pipers at the *Grand Festival de Cornouaille*

Brittany

Brittany has a jagged coast with many rocky headlands and islets. It resembles Cornwall or New England, with fishing villages and small resorts on the sandy inlets of its rugged coast. One estuary is called Aber Vrach. An example of the similarity of the ancient Celtic languages still spoken in Brittany and Wales is that *aber* in Breton means "estuary", as it does in Welsh. Many Breton churches are dedicated to Welsh saints, and some of the songs and dances are similar. Bretons play a bag-pipe, very like the Scottish one.

Brittany is a region of interesting local costumes and festivals. In July there is the *Grand Festival de Cornouaille* at Quimper in southwestern Brittany. Cornouaille was settled by Celts driven from British Cornwall by the Saxons about A D 600, hence the similarity of the names Cornwall and Cornouaille. Another famous festival is that of the Blue Nets at Concarneau in August, so called because the fishermen's sardine-catching nets are blue.

Calvary at Plougastèl

Inland, Brittany is called *Ar-coat* in Breton, meaning "the wood", for it was once forested. Now there are pastures and cider-apple orchards, lined by hedges as in England, as well as many heather and gorse covered moors. The local churches often have huge stone calvaries outside, with one or more crucifixes surrounded by statues telling the story of the Life of Jesus.

In the past most Bretons were fishermen and part-time farmers. Fleets of cod fishing boats sailed to Newfoundland from St. Malo. But many fishermen have long since turned to full-time vegetable farming. The climate is mild and they can earn good money by growing early potatoes, cauliflowers and onions for sale in northern France and Britain. The land once was barren and rocky, but the farmers have enclosed their fields with walls or hedges and fertilized the soil.

Onion stall on the outskirts of St. Brieuc

42

Fishing is still important in some parts of Brittany. Lobster boats sail from Douarnenez to fish off the British Isles, and sardine and lobster boats go on voyages of two or three weeks to fish the seas around Spain and Morocco. From Concarneau tuna fleets sail to North and West African waters. Both Douarnenez and Concarneau have modern warehouses for sorting, packing and canning fish.

Many tourists visit Brittany in summer. At first people stayed in fishermen's or farmers' houses, but a few towns such as Dinard and La Baule developed for visitors, and today tourism is the main occupation of the many little towns and villages along the coast. Visitors come to enjoy the scenery and sandy beaches, to see the Breton costumes and dances, and to eat the local specialities—lobsters, oysters, mussels and crayfish. Another local speciality is a creamy sauce made from shellfish. Food served with it is called *à l'Armoricain*, from *armor*, the Breton word for "sea".

Each district of Brittany has its headdress

Tourists bring money to Brittany, but only in the summer. The government is encouraging new industries in the region, and there is a modern Citroen car factory at Rennes.

Across the Rance estuary, near St. Malo and Dinard, is a dam with the world's first tidal power station. It was built here because the difference between high and low tides is as much as 44 feet, and also there are two high and two low tides every 25 hours. Incoming and outgoing tides move propellers which turn 24 turbines to generate electricity.

Tidal barrage on the Rance

43

Large modern school at St. Flour

Schools

French schools are very different from those in Britain or America. Classes last from eight o'clock or quarter past eight until twelve, and from two o'clock until four or five o'clock. Then there is much homework for secondary-school students, especially in the *lycées* or grammar schools. Thursdays are usually free in primary schools, but secondary-school pupils have only Thursday or Saturday afternoon, as well as Sunday.

Lessons are more like lectures from the teacher, especially for older pupils, and children are kept in order by a non-teacher *censeur* and young *surveillants*. Classes are often large with between 40 and 50 pupils and schools commonly have 2000 or more pupils.

Education is very competitive. There are tests each week and term in every subject. Anyone who does not always pass may not be allowed to continue in that class or school.

There are private and state schools, but all teach the same subjects and have identical courses of study for pupils of the same age. State schools are run by the central government, not by local councils as in Britain or America. The ministry of education decides almost everything about schools—dates of holidays, what shall be taught, when and how.

Many pupils between the ages of 11 and 15 now go to comprehensive secondary or junior high schools. They follow a "classics", "modern", "traditional" or "terminal" course. At 15 or 16 they will either leave, or go to a senior high school to be trained either for industry, commerce or university entrance. The *Baccalauréat* at 17 or 18 years is a very stiff examination for those leaving school and likely to go to a university or college.

There are few school clubs or societies. Most schools have none, but some are being started. There is a little physical education but few team games, so matches with other schools are rare. The whole aim of school in France is to teach facts and ideas, and to train pupils to think.

The French have a tremendous respect for education, teachers and the well-spoken.

Parisian schoolboys on their way home from school

Urdos, near the
Spanish border

The Pyrenees

The Pyrenees form an impressive mountain barrier between France and Spain. They rise sharply on the French side and there are almost no easy passes across them, so the main routes into Spain keep to the coasts. The people of each valley formed separate communities, each with its own capital and market. The semi-independent state of Andorra still has its own laws and general council and its own postage stamps.

The Basques live in the westernmost Pyrenees, both in France and Spain. Their homeland is very rainy so there are many rushing rivers, called *gaves*. There are also many trees, although fewer than in past centuries. Sheep graze on the short grass of the limestone pasturelands and their milk is made into Roquefort cheese.

The Basque language is strangely unlike any other European language. The Basque people also have their own dances, such as the *fandango* and the *arinarin*, and their national game is *pelota*. Pelota is played with a hard, leather-covered ball against a wall called a *fronton* using bare hands or a *chistera*, a long curved basket. The Basques have given the world (and especially the French) one part of their national costume— the beret.

46

To the east the Pyrenees are at their highest and most Alpine. The valleys have been deepened by glaciers, which have also hollowed out huge round *cirques*, or amphitheatres, such as the tremendous Cirque de Gavarnie, whose steep sides rise 5000 feet. The upper waters of the *gaves* supply hydro-electric power. Skiers

Basque dancers

come here in winter, and people who are ill go to one of the spas in summer. Many pilgrims visit Lourdes and the limestone grotto with its famous spring which is believed by some to have miraculous powers of healing.

The ridges of the easternmost Pyrenees open out towards the sea like outstretched fingers. Catalans live here, as well as across the border in Spain, and speak their own Spanish-type dialect.

Mont Louis, a border fortress built by Louis XIV's military engineer Vauban, now houses an experimental furnace using solar energy. From Mont Louis down the Conflent (river Tet) to the sea, one passes through ever warmer and drier parts of the valley. High up there are pines and pasturelands, then hardy fruit trees such as apples and pears, then fruit bushes. Lower still come apricots and almonds, then peaches, then vines, and lastly irrigated *huertas* or market gardens where fruits and vegetables such as peaches, apricots and lettuces are cultivated.

There are coves on the rocky Roussillon coast in which lie small towns such as picturesque Collioure and wine-producing Banyuls.

Collioure

47

Aiguille Verte

Alps and Jura

From Lake Geneva to the Mediterranean most of the Alps are in France, and their landscapes are more varied than elsewhere. The finest scenery and the highest mountains are near the Italian border, especially in the massifs of Mont Blanc, Vanoise and Pelvoux. These lofty peaks were chiselled by mighty glaciers in the Ice Ages. Some glaciers remain, but they are shrinking.

A spectacular way of seeing the peaks and glaciers is to take the *téléphérique*, or cable-car service, across the Alps from Chamonix in France to Courmayeur in Italy. Standing in a cabin holding a hundred passengers and rising at 15 mph, one passes over the Bossons glacier. On one side is Mont Blanc, on the other side the Aiguille Verte, and across the valley the Aiguilles Massif. At over 9000 feet one changes to a fifty-passenger cabin to rise another 6000 feet in a two-mile journey at 25 mph. The cables are unsupported by pylons and hang just in front of the near-vertical face of the Aiguille du Midi. From here the Pèlerins glacier and the entrance to the world's longest road tunnel (7 miles from Chamonix to Courmayeur) can be seen far below. At over 15,000 feet one is very near the peak of the Aiguille du Midi. Skiers can descend from here into the Vallée Blanche—a snowfield over a glacier—at any time of the year.

But it can be crossed in 4-seater cabins on the *téléphérique*. Here one is in the middle of the Mont Blanc Massif and its snowfields. It is like crossing part of Greenland.

At the Pointe Helbronner, 13,495 feet, is the Franco-Italian border, with passport and customs control. This is the watershed between the Rhône river and the Po river in Italy.

Climbers on Mont Blanc

Alpine chalet. The train is just entering an avalanche shelter

West of the High Alps is a great arc-shaped valley over 100 miles long. Many smaller valleys from the High Alps run into it, and roads and railways have been built along it. The mountains on either side shelter the valley so well that maize (or corn), tobacco and vines grow well. The rivers flood quickly when the snow melts each year, so farmers do not use land close to them.

Grenoble, in the middle of the valley and of the Alps, was the capital of the old province of Dauphiné. This was sold to France in 1349 on condition that the heir to the French throne would be called *Le Dauphin*. Grenoble is a rapidly developing industrial city, mainly because it was the first place in the world where hydro-electric power was developed (1868–89). French hydro-electric-power engineers are still among the best in the world and, although they can no longer boast of having the world's largest dam, they are still at the forefront of modern developments with their tidal power station in Brittany.

Cattle graze on high Alpine pastures in summer, while the grass in the valleys is cut for hay to feed the animals indoors in the winter. The milk is brought down to the valleys on simple aerial ropeways and sometimes even by pipelines. Gruyère cheese is made in large dairies, as it is in the Jura, but individual farmers make other local cheeses, such as Savoy Tomme, which is covered with grape pips, or seeds, and Mt. Cenis which is made from a mixture of sheep and cows' milk.

In the westernmost Pre-Alps are the beautiful lakes of Annecy and Le Bourget, and the famous spa of Aix-les-Bains where people still come to take special baths in the mineral springs as a cure for rheumatism. To the south in High Provence almost all the Alps are bare limestone, worn away by wind, rain and extremes of heat and cold. Water is scarce and pastures are good enough only for sheep. There are few trees, so farms are built of stone, instead of the timber used in the Alps to the north. This is a land of biting winter winds and glaring summer sun, and many of the people who once lived here have left to work on the Mediterranean or in the Rhône valley.

The Franche-Comté, or land of the Jura, was for long fought over between the French and Austrians. It became French in 1678, but the Jura mountains are still divided between France and Switzerland.

Lake Annecy

51

Folk dancing at Montbéliard

Pipe-maker at St. Claude

The western Jura are poor, wind-swept and cut by rivers, some of which disappear underground. Besançon, the old Franche-Comté capital, has an important watch-making industry. Near Montbéliard at Audincourt are the Peugeot car and motor-cycle factories. Peugeot is one of the best known of French cars, and many are sold abroad.

In the narrow but sheltered valleys of the eastern Jura even grapes grow well. The chemist Louis Pasteur worked in this region, at Arbois, on diseases of the vine. He is best known for his work on pasteurization in which liquids are heated to a temperature high enough to kill the bacteria they contain. This process is used today to kill the germs in milk.

Jura comes from a Latin word (*juria*) meaning "forest", and timber still provides one of the region's main sources of income. It is used for fuel, for making toys and souvenirs, and for building the large, low-roofed chalets typical of this part of France. There are also hundreds of small workshops in homes and sheds, where parts of watches, projectors, micro-scopes, spectacles and smokers' pipes are made—to be sent for assembly to towns such as Morez and St. Claude.

Pont du Gard
aqueduct

The Saône-Rhône Valley

The Saône-Rhône valley was one of the great trade routes of history. Tin from Cornwall and Brittany was taken by this route in the fourth century BC to supply Greek and Roman bronze foundries. Amber from the Baltic also passed this way to the Mediterranean and the Orient. Up the valleys came the Romans, founding Gaul and countless towns. In the valleys they left magnificent relics such as the triple-arcaded Pont du Gard aqueduct. Along the valleys now pass France's busiest railway and road, linking northern and southern Europe as well as France. All this is possible because of two other routes at the head of the Saône valley—one giving easy passage to the Rhine, the other leading to Lorraine, Paris and the Low Countries.

South of Dijon are Burgundy's vineyards, rarely over a mile wide and usually 5 to 10 acres in extent. They lie halfway down a gentle slope on the west bank of the Saône. From *La Côte d'Or*, "the golden edge", come Burgundy's greatest wines. As in Champagne, soil and sunny slopes are happily combined. One of the most famous vineyards is Clos Vougeot. Many years ago a general made his troops present arms when passing it, and a pope created a cardinal of a priest who sent him thirty barrels of its wine.

Wine cellars at Le Clos Vougeot

Beaune, like Reims, is honeycombed with wine cellars. The Hôtel Dieu, or hospital for the poor, was founded fifty years before Columbus discovered America. Over the years vineyards have been given to this charity, and its income is mainly from the wine which these produce. Wine auctions are held each November in its courtyard.

Farther south the wine is usually less outstanding and most is sold as Beaujolais, the name of the region around Mâcon. So much wine is produced in Burgundy that one can appreciate the local saying, "Three rivers bathe Lyons, the Saône, the Rhône and the Beaujolais."

The Romans built Lugdunum, capital of Gaul, high on a hill near where the Rhône and Saône join. Later known as Lyons, it became famous through its annual fair, started in 1420 and still held, and through its silk industry brought here by Italian refugees. Fine silk cloth is still made in small workshops in the Croix-Rousse quarter, and in many towns in the district. Other textiles are also made, and the dye-stuffs needed gave rise to a chemical industry. There are many other industries in this third city of France, which has well over half a million people, and a reputation for the best food of any French city.

The hospice at Beaune

54

Windbreak of poplars, rushes and canes

The bridge at Avignon

South of Lyons there were many famous vineyards until a century ago when the disease phylloxera killed most of the vines. Now only a few are left, around Vienne, Valence and Avignon. Farmers in the region have turned to intensive fruit and vegetable farming, including melons at Cavaillon and peaches at Avignon. But this part of France is sometimes hit by the *mistral*. This is a bitingly cold and furious wind, and is especially dangerous in spring and early summer, when it can kill new and tender crops. So tall cypresses are grown as windbreaks, reinforced by reeds, rushes and fences. There are also automatic heaters in the fields, which turn on when the temperature falls dangerously low.

Montélimar is famous for nougat, and Orange is the original home of the House of Orange, the Dutch royal family. Farther downstream is Avignon, a famous town with medieval walls and the old Palace of the Popes, who lived here from 1309 to 1377. Above the palace a rock overlooks the Rhône and the broken footbridge across the river. This is the bridge of the song: *"Sur le pont d'Avignon, on y danse . . ."* The bridge is really too narrow for dancing in a ring but people sometimes dance to the song under its arches.

The Palace of the Popes

Inside the Roman arena at Arles

Arles, at first a Greek settlement, was later a leading Roman city, and in the fifth century A D was one of the world's greatest markets. The Romans built a canal to the sea avoiding the marshy delta, a pontoon bridge over the Rhône to carry their road from Italy to Spain, and the arena still used for bull fights.

The Camargue, or Rhône Delta, was once a wilderness of lagoons, sand, flamingo, bulls and horsemen. Now it is becoming dominated by rice fields, although part is a nature preserve or sanctuary.

Aigues-Mortes, on the west side of the delta, is still enclosed within its perfect medieval walls. Louis IX (St. Louis) started from here in 1248 on his crusade to Jerusalem, but the town is now some 5 miles from the sea. Yet salt water is still brought in by canal for salt pans which have been producing salt for 1200 years.

The turbulent Rhône is being tamed for power, navigation and irrigation and the Rhône Valley is France's most rapidly developing industrial region. Some of Europe's largest power stations have been built here. Near one, between Donzère and Mondragon, are factories making radioactive isotopes; and at Marcoule is France's first nuclear power station, opened in 1956.

Street in Aigues Mortes

56

Mediterranean

At the eastern end of the Aquitaine Basin a strip of lowland squeezes between the Massif Central and the Pyrenees, and opens out into the Mediterranean plain of Languedoc. To command this routeway Gauls, Romans, Visigoths and Franks built Carcassonne. This is Europe's best preserved fortress, over a mile in circumference, with a town in and around it. The Canal du Midi passes Carcassonne. It was built in the seventeenth century to link the Atlantic with the Mediterranean, but it is little used today.

There were vast areas of vineyards in Languedoc, which produced more ordinary red wine than could be sold. So a canal has been built to bring water to irrigate more valuable crops such as peaches and vegetables.

Years ago people kept away from the lagoon-lined and marshy coast because of the mosquitoes which carried malaria. But now that the marshes have been drained the mosquitoes have disappeared and, with help from the government, seaside resorts are being built. There will be places for yachting and camping, as well as traditional villas and hotels.

Aix-en-Provence, the market square

Musician in Marseilles band

East of the Rhône, mountains come down to the Mediterranean, contrasting with its azure sea and protecting most of the coast from the chilly *mistral* wind. Little over a hundred years ago few people lived along this coast. In earlier centuries pirates often attacked it, so most towns were on hills away from the sea and from the mosquitoes. Aix-en-Provence, the old capital and modern town, is well inland.

Nice is an old coastal town, but Cannes is more typical of the seaside holiday resorts. The town's development dates from 1834 when Lord Brougham, then Lord Chancellor of England, was unable to stay in Nice because of the cholera there. So he stayed instead in the tiny fishing village of Cannes. He liked it so much that he built a house there, which he visited for the next thirty-four winters. He was soon followed by many British aristocrats escaping the English winter. Today thousands of visitors come throughout the year to the almost continual line of coastal resorts which make up the *Côte d'Azur*. In winter the weather is pleasantly mild, while in summer continuous sun is the rule.

Local foods are very different on this coast from those elsewhere in France. Olive oil is used for cooking instead of butter, and garlic is added to most dishes. *Bouillabaisse*, a stew

58

of many kinds of fish with onions, tomatoes, herbs and wine, is very popular. So are fish soups, shellfish and *ratatouille*—different kinds of vegetables cut up and fried together in oil.

Marseilles is an excellent place to try these and other dishes, especially in restaurants along the famous street *La Canebière* and near the *Vieux Port* (old port).

During its long history Marseilles has flourished most in the last two centuries—through trade with Africa and the Orient. But there is little flat land, especially near the sea, so piers and a protective breakwater had to be built into the harbour for the merchant shipping. Eventually even these were not enough, and in the 1930's the Rove Canal was built in a tunnel under a high ridge to the Etang de Berre, an inlet of the sea to the northwest. The oil refineries and petro-chemical works of Marseilles are here. Now space again is short, and tankers are getting larger, so new docks and industries are being developed at Fos, farther to the west.

Fishermen at Marseilles selling their catch

Marseilles is France's second city (though it has only one-quarter the population of Paris), and in most respects it is the first port. Some trade has declined — Marseilles is now far from Europe's main industrial areas. Some people have called it "France's backdoor", but it would prefer to be known as "the Europort of the South".

This red cow with a black head was painted on the cave walls at Lascaux about 15,000 years ago

History

Man first lived in France over 20,000 years ago, and some early inhabitants painted animals on cave walls. Stone pillars, slabs and tombs, famous in Brittany, were put up by peoples who came 2000 years before Christ. The Romans founded many cities, and built roads, aqueducts and open-air theatres.

Roman rule collapsed, but four centuries later, in the eighth century, Charlemagne tried to revive it and united most of France, Germany and Italy. When he died, his three sons divided the empire, and the French lands were soon invaded by the Normans. Both Norman and English kings ruled in turn on both sides of the Channel. Gradually, by war or marriage between rulers, France was united under rather autocratic rulers, of whom Louis XIV was, perhaps, the most famous.

Hatred of such rule and bad conditions led to the French Revolution of 1789, when many aristocrats lost their lives. The First Republic was declared in 1792; Louis XVI was tried and executed in the following year.

Napoleon Bonaparte, a general in the First Republic, tried to liberate all Europe from autocratic rulers but became one himself, proclaiming himself emperor. However, he left France with more roads and bridges, codes of law and administration, and its school system.

Louis XIV

Napoleon I

When Napoleon's empire was overthrown, France went back to kings—first one branch of the royal family, the Bourbons, then another, the Orleans. A further revolution in 1848 brought in the Second Republic. Napoleon III, nephew of Bonaparte, soon abolished that and became a feeble dictator. When he was defeated by the Prussians in the Franco-Prussian war of 1870, there was another extremely bloody revolution in Paris, but the Third Republic (1871) survived until World War II, though with many changes of government.

In 1940 the whole of northern France and the Atlantic coast was occupied by the Germans. Just before the fall of Paris, the government moved south, eventually becoming established at Vichy where, with Marshal Pétain as Head of State, it ruled under the occupying Germans. During this period, many Frenchmen joined an underground Resistance movement against the Germans, and General Charles de Gaulle escaped to London where he placed himself at the head of the "Free French" forces who joined him in exile.

The Liberation of France in 1945 brought the Fourth Republic with de Gaulle as its head but, because of later conflict between ministers, he resigned in 1946. Many brief governments followed until 1958, when the Fifth Republic was created with de Gaulle as its President. The new constitution gave parliament and ministers less power. President de Gaulle had more power than previous presidents, but was not a dictator. He worked to make France influential in the world and his country stronger economically. During his presidency independence was granted to Algeria and the African colonies, although French economic interest is still strong in most of them.

Ski lesson in the Alps

Sport

A few decades ago the French were less interested in sports, except for fishing and shooting, than the British or Americans. That has all changed.

Bicycle racing is, however, an old sport. The annual *Tour de France* was first held in 1903, in the early days of bicycles. Competitors have 20 day-long races in succession, each of about 150 hilly miles. Crowds watch them rush through towns with heads down and bottoms up.

Now there is more interest in car racing. The Monte Carlo International Rally, held each January, starts at various points in Europe. Drivers converge on France's mountains at the worst time of the year. The Le Mans race is 24 hours with a course around a track and on ordinary roads.

Football (soccer) is the most popular sport to play and watch. The *Coupe de France* is the French Cup Final. Rugby, with fifteen players, is mostly played in southern France. A national team participates in Rugby Internationals against England, Wales, Scotland and Ireland.

The French government is now providing special places where young people can practise sports. France is now doing better in Olympic athletics, and she has always done well in skiing. A Frenchman, Pierre de Coubertin, helped found the modern Olympic Games.

Skiing is one of the most popular sports. France is fortunate in having many sunny snowfields, especially in the Alps. In some places one can ski throughout the year. More and more schools send whole classes with their teachers to the mountains for a month. They have ordinary lessons before or after lunch, and skiing instruction in the other half of the day. A young Frenchman, Jean-Claude Killy, won three gold medals for skiing in the 1968 Winter Olympics.

Sailing is the fastest growing summer sport, more so even than tennis. There are so many yachts that at least one resort has a 90-minute mooring limit. Under-water swimming and diving have become popular because of the exploits of Jacques Yves Cousteau, the co-inventor of the aqua lung.

Basketball is played by both sexes, and volley-ball was introduced to France by American troops in World War I. Boxing, wrestling and judo are all popular.

Pelota is played in the Basque country and *boules* (bowls) is a southern game which has become national. Bull fighting (usually without killing the bulls) is seen in the south.

Playing *pelota*

63

Index

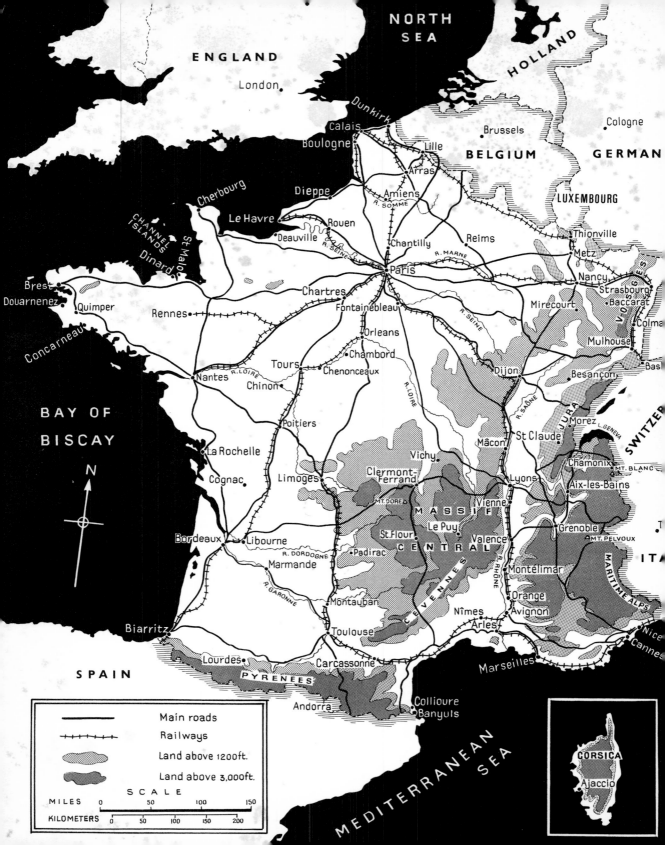

DATE DUE

SEP 29 '71		
OCT 4 '72		
APR 1 1 '73		
SEP 2 4 '73		
AUG 2 5 '77		
JUN 2 8 '90		
JAN 2 2 '94		
GAYLORD		PRINTED IN U.S.A.